fill a bucket

A Guide to Daily Happiness for Young Children

By Carol McCloud and Katherine Martin, M.A.

Illustrated by David Messing

 Bucket Fillosophy

Bucket Fillosophy®

Bucket Fillosophy® is an imprint of Bucket Fillers, Inc.
PO Box 255, Brighton, MI 48116 • (810) 229-5468
www.bucketfillers101.com

Authors' Acknowledgments

In the 1960s, Dr. Donald O. Clifton (1924-2003) first created the "Dipper and Bucket" story that has now been passed along for decades. Dr. Clifton later went on to co-author the #1 *New York Times* bestseller *How Full is Your Bucket?* and was named the Father of Strengths Psychology.

A portion of the proceeds from this book is being donated to the Methodist Children's Home Society in Redford, Michigan, an organization which has served abused and neglected children for more than one hundred years.

Copyright © 2008, 2017 by Carol McCloud

Illustrated by David Messing.
Redesigned by Glenn Zimmer.
Edited by Kathleen Marusak.

Library of Congress Cataloging-in-Publication Data

Names: McCloud, Carol and Martin, Katherine. | Messing, David, illustrator.
Title: Fill a bucket : a guide to daily happiness for young children / by Carol McCloud and Katherine Martin ; illustrated by David Messing.
Description: Brighton, MI : Bucket Fillosophy, 2017. | Summary: The concept of a full bucket is an effective metaphor for a child's healthy self-concept and happiness, most often the result of encouraging words and actions of parents and others who help a child know they are loved, valued, and capable.
Identifiers: LCCN 2016918056 (print) | ISBN 9780996099974 (paperback) | ISBN 9780996099981 (hardcover) | ISBN 9781945369063, 9781945369070, 9781945369087 (ebooks)
Subjects: BISAC: JUVENILE NONFICTION / Social Topics / Self-Esteem & Self-Reliance. | JUVENILE NONFICTION / Social Topics / Bullying.
LC record available at https://lccn.loc.gov/2008929764
Printed in the United States on recycled paper.
10 9 8 7 6 5 4 3

fill a bucket®

Tune: *Frère Jacques* or *Are You Sleeping?*

1. Fill a buck – et Eve – ry day
2. Fill a buck – et Eve – ry day

I can fill a buck - et You can too
I like fill–ing buck – ets You will too

1. Fill a bucket. (Fill a bucket.)
   Every day. (Every day.)
   I can fill a bucket. (I can fill a bucket.)
   You can too. (You can too.)

2. Fill a bucket. (Fill a bucket.)
   Every day. (Every day.)
   I like filling buckets. (I like filling buckets.)
   You will too. (You will too.)

3

The day you were born was a very happy day.
It was your birthday, a day you celebrate every year.

You were a new person and a special gift. You received a gift too—your very own name, a name as special as you. What is your name?

Everyone was so happy to see you.
But, there was one part of you that they could not see.
It was your bucket, your invisible bucket.

Everyone is born with an invisible bucket. No one can see our bucket, but it is always with you. Your bucket is a very important part of you. It is an important part of everyone.

Your bucket holds all the love and happiness you receive
each day. When your bucket is full, you feel happy.
When your bucket is empty, you feel sad.
It's good to have a full bucket.

Every day, your family and lots of other people help fill
your bucket. When your daddy kisses and tickles you,
he fills your bucket. Your giggles fill his bucket, too.

When your mommy smiles and tells you she loves you, she is filling your bucket. Your smiles fill her bucket, too.

When your sister or your brother snuggles and reads to you,
your buckets fill up even more.

When your grandpa or your grandma plays with you,
everyone's bucket is filled.

Look! Your bucket is so full! It is full of happy thoughts and lots of love. So many people have filled your bucket. You can fill their buckets, too.

Bucket filling is like magic. When you fill a bucket by being kind and loving, your bucket fills up, too.

You can do so many things to fill buckets every day.
When you listen and help, you are filling a bucket.
Your bucket fills up more.

15

When you say "please" and "thank you,"
your magic words fill buckets.

When you play and share your toys, everyone is happy.
Everyone's invisible bucket is filled.

When you take care of your pet, you are filling a bucket.
Your bucket fills up, too.

When you smile and wave to those you see,
you are being a bucket filler.

When you give hugs and kisses, your love fills buckets. It's good to go to sleep with a bucket full of happiness and love

Look! Look at all the happy faces.
Everyone's bucket is full.

Now it's your turn.

What can you do to fill a bucket today?

About the Authors

Carol McCloud, the Bucket Lady, and her Bucket Fillers Team teach the importance of bucket filling to educators, businesses, community groups, churches, and children. As an early childhood specialist, Carol understands that patterns affecting self-worth start very early in life and are fostered by others. Carol is president of Bucket Fillers, Inc., an educational organization in Brighton, Michigan, whose mission is to create bucketfilling families, schools, workplaces, and communities. She lives in Venice, Florida with her husband, Jack. **Visit www.bucketfillers101.com.**

Katherine Martin has an M.A. in Counseling with a Specialization in Child and Adolescence. Kathy has extensive experience in family counseling, including grief counseling and suicide prevention. She has designed and directed activities and educational programs for both youth and seniors and is currently working in the field of special education.

About the Illustrator

David Messing is a life-long artist, illustrator, cartoonist, sculptor, writer and instructor. For thirty years, Dave, along with his wife Sandy, and in more recent years, their boys Scott, Kevin and Adam, have taught in their family-owned art school. Although Dave spent many years designing and building props, sets, and miniatures for film and print commercials and almost every auto manufacturer, his current passion is cartooning and book illustration. **Visit www.davidmessingstudio.com.**